Contents

Any words appearing in the text in bold, **like this**, are explained in the Glossary.

Who was Barbara Hepworth?

Barbara Hepworth was a great modern artist. She was a famous **sculptor**. In Hepworth's time, this was a very unusual thing for a woman to be.

Although Hepworth was a leading English sculptor, she also produced many paintings and drawings.

sculpture

Barbara Hepworth with one of her sculptures.

4

TAKE-OFF!

The Life and Work of ...

Barbara Hepworth

WARWICKSHIRE
COUNTY LIBRARY

CONTROL No.

Jayne Woodhouse

Heinemann

www.heinemann.co.uk/library
Visit our website to find out more information about Heinemann Library books.

To order:

 Phone 44 (0) 1865 888066

 Send a fax to 44 (0) 1865 314091

 Visit the Heinemann Bookshop at www.heinemann.co.uk/library to browse our catalogue and order online.

First published in Great Britain by Heinemann Library, Halley Court, Jordan Hill, Oxford OX2 8EJ, a division of Reed Educational and Professional Publishing Ltd. Heinemann is a registered trademark of Reed Educational and Professional Publishing Ltd.

OXFORD MELBOURNE AUCKLAND JOHANNESBURG BLANTYRE
GABORONE IBADAN PORTSMOUTH (NH) USA CHICAGO

Designed by Celia Floyd
Originated by Dot Gradations Ltd
Printed and bound by South China Printing in Hong Kong/China

ISBN 0 431 13160 0 (hardback)   ISBN 0 431 13165 1 (paperback)
06 05 04 03 02   06 05 04 03 02
10 9 8 7 6 5 4 3 2 1   10 9 8 7 6 5 4 3 2 1

British Library Cataloguing in Publication Data

Woodhouse, Jayne
  The life and work of Barbara Hepworth
  1. Hepworth, Barbara, 1903–1975
  2. Women sculptors — England – Biography – Juvenile literature
  3. Sculptors – England – Biography – Juvenile literature
  4. Sculpture – England – Juvenile literature
  I. Title II. Barbara Hepworth
  730.9'2

Acknowledgements

The publishers would like to thank the following for permission to reproduce photographs: Alan Bowness, Hepworth Estate: pp4, 10, 13, 22, 23, 24, 27; Andrew Besley: p28; Bridgeman Art Library: p9; Hulton Getty: pp8, 14; John Cleare Mountain Photography: p6; Popperfoto: p26; Robert Harding Picture Library: p18; Science Photo Library: p20; Scottish National Gallery of Modern Art: p5; Tate Archive: pp12, 16; Tate Gallery, St Ives: p29; Tate Picture Library: pp7, 11, 15, 17, 19, 21, 25.

Cover photograph: Three figures from the *Family of Man. Ancestor I, Ancestor II* and *Parent I, c.* 1970 (bronze), reproduced with permission of Bridgeman/Fitzwilliam Museum.

All Hepworth works of art copyright © Alan Bowness, Hepworth Estate.

Our thanks to Sue Graves and Hilda Reed for their advice and expertise in the preparation of this book.

Every effort has been made to contact copyright holders of any material reproduced in this book. Any omissions will be rectified in subsequent printings if notice is given to the publishers.

Hepworth's most important **sculptures** are **abstract art**. They are made from wood, stone and, later, **bronze**. Hepworth said her work was a way of 'holding a beautiful thought'.

hollowed space

wires

Wave, 1943–44

Can you see the fine wires that have been stretched across this sculpture?

Early years

Barbara Hepworth was born in Wakefield, Yorkshire, on 10 January 1903. Some of her earliest memories were of the countryside there. She never forgot the shapes made by the roads, hills and fields.

Countryside like this influenced Hepworth's work.

hill

field

Even as a small child Barbara Hepworth knew that she wanted to be a **sculptor**.

All her life, Hepworth was inspired by nature and the landscape. This **sculpture** shows how she saw the waves breaking on the beach.

Barbara made this **bronze** sculpture in 1958 when she lived by the sea.

Sea Form (Porthmeor), 1958

Learning to be an artist

When Barbara was only 17, she went to Leeds School of Art. There she met the **sculptor Henry Moore**, who shared many of her ideas. One year later, Barbara entered the Royal College of Art in London.

Henry Moore and one of his sculptures at Leeds School of Art.

Barbara first learnt to carve in stone during a visit to Italy in 1924. Her early works were simple figures of people, animals and birds, like this pair of doves.

Hepworth said she always knew what the final shape of a **sculpture** would be even before she began working on it.

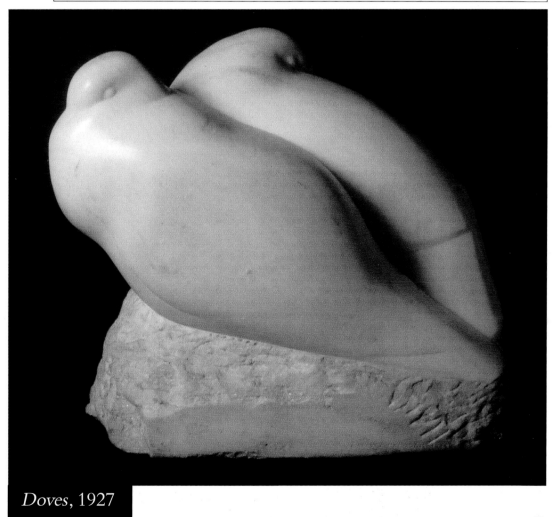

Doves, 1927

Motherhood

While she was in Italy, Barbara married John Skeaping. He was another British **sculptor**. They returned to London in 1926. Three years later, their son Paul was born.

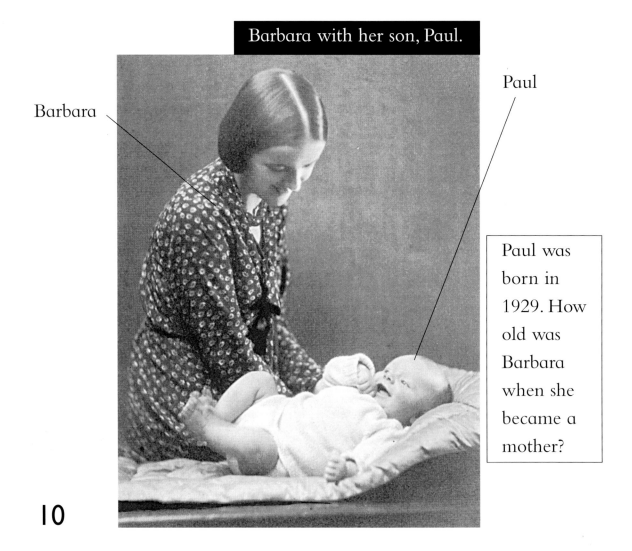

Barbara with her son, Paul.

Barbara

Paul

Paul was born in 1929. How old was Barbara when she became a mother?

10

While the baby lay in his cot or on a rug nearby,
Barbara would go on with her carving.

Barbara made this figure of Paul sleeping.
It is made out of hard, dark wood.

— dark wood

Infant, 1929

Changing ideas

From 1930, Hepworth began to explore **abstract art**. Her **sculptures** no longer looked like things in real life. Instead, they showed her ideas about shape and space.

Hepworth working in her studio.

sculpture

Hepworth used **textures** and shapes in her sculptures to show feelings and moods.

Hepworth was one of the first artists to carve holes right through the stone. She used this idea many times.

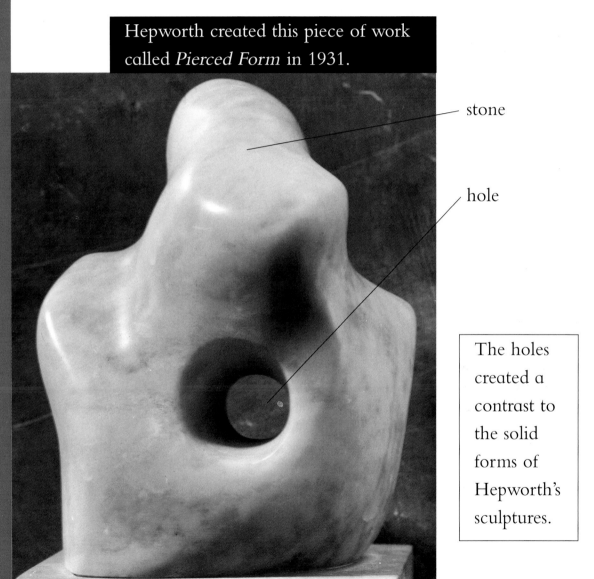

Hepworth created this piece of work called *Pierced Form* in 1931.

stone

hole

The holes created a contrast to the solid forms of Hepworth's sculptures.

A new family

In 1931, Barbara Hepworth met the **abstract** painter Ben Nicholson. He became her second husband. In 1934, Hepworth gave birth to triplets.

Barbara   Ben Nicholson

Barbara Hepworth with her second husband.

The arrival of her three babies gave Hepworth new ideas. She began to make pieces of work in groups of three. This one is **carved** from white **marble**.

Three Forms, 1935

Hepworth often worked until her arms ached and her fingers were bleeding!

Working life

It was not always easy for Hepworth to be an artist and a mother. She often had very little time to work. Her **studio** was sometimes a jumble of rocks, **sculptures**, children and washing!

Hepworth in her studio.

However, Hepworth said that her children were always an important **inspiration** to her. In the 1930s, she made several works based on the idea of a mother and child.

mother   child

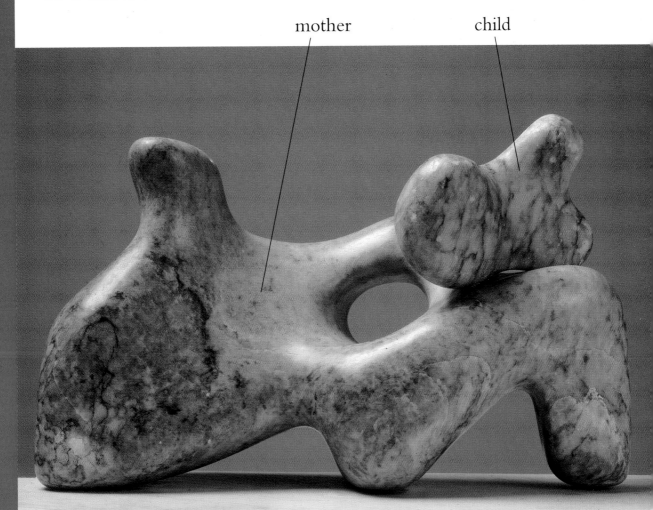

Mother and Child, 1934

St Ives

When World War II began in 1939, Barbara Hepworth and her family moved from London to St Ives in Cornwall. Hepworth loved the Cornish **landscape** with its rocky cliffs, sea and bright light.

rocks   lighthouse   sea

Part of the Cornish coastline.

Hepworth called this piece *Pelagos*, which is the Greek word for the sea. It was **inspired** by the view of the land and the waves from her **studio** window. It is made of partly-painted wood and strings.

You can see this sculpture in the Tate Modern (**Gallery**), London.

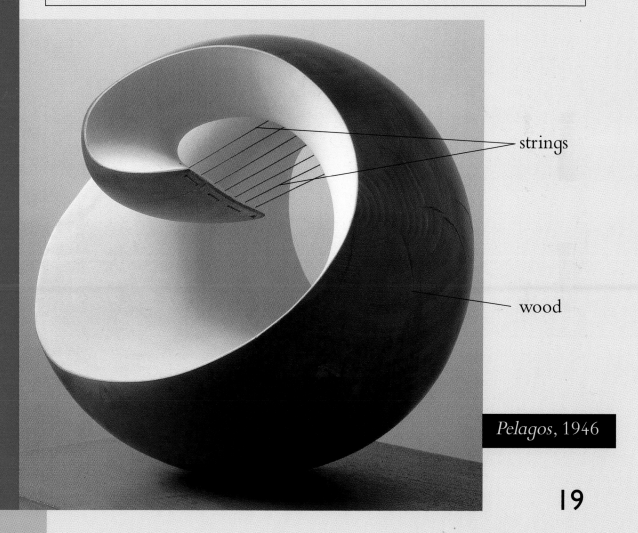

strings

wood

Pelagos, 1946

Different ways of working

Paintings and drawings were also part of Hepworth's work. In the 1940s, she made several visits to hospitals. There she watched operations being carried out.

surgeon

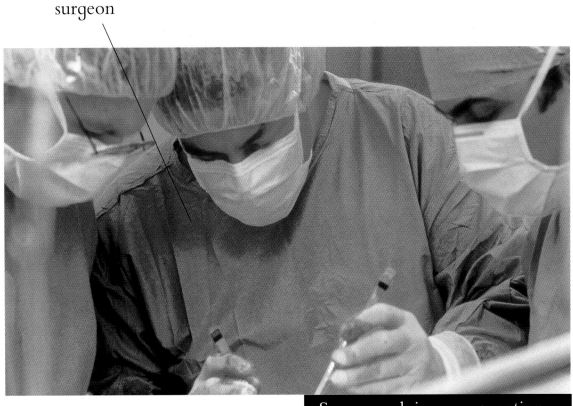

Surgeons doing an operation.

The Scalpel, 1949

This drawing is based on **sketches** Hepworth made in a hospital **operating theatre**. To her, the way the doctors and nurses worked together seemed like a kind of **sculpture**.

Large forms

In 1949, Hepworth bought Trewyn **Studio** in St Ives. She lived there for the rest of her life. For the first time, she had enough space to make really large **sculptures**.

Hepworth   large sculptures

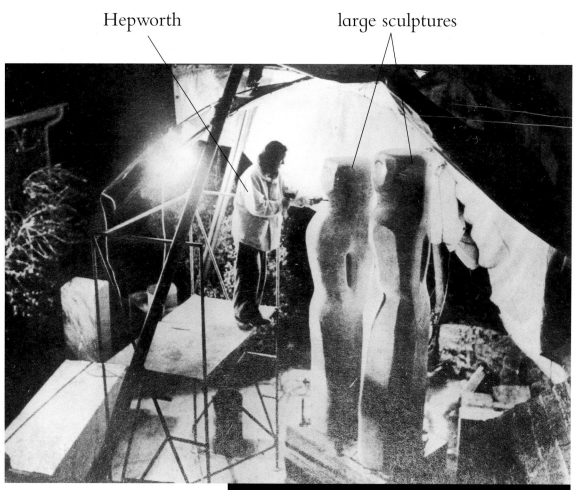

Hepworth in the Trewyn Studio, St Ives.

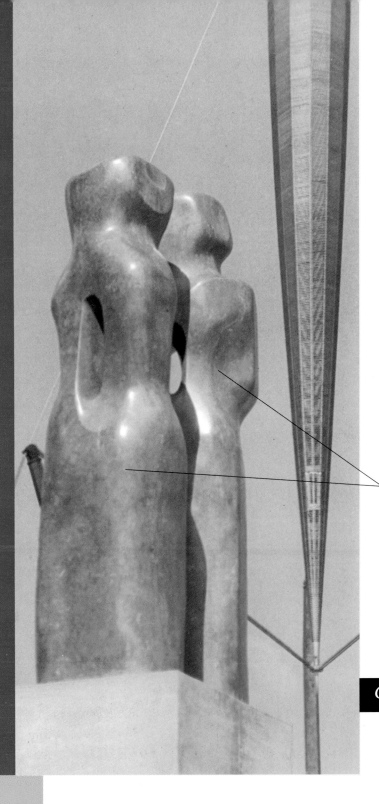

Some of Hepworth's large pieces of work were based on human figures. They were made to be seen outside, as part of the **landscape**, not in an art **gallery**.

sculpted figures

Contrapuntal Forms, 1951

23

New materials

From the 1950s, Hepworth began to work in **bronze**. First she made the sculpture in plaster. Then a **mould** was made of it, into which she poured hot bronze.

shape

Hepworth

Hepworth and two assistants create a shape for the sculpture.

assistants

This finished **sculpture** is called *Four-Square (Walk Through)*. It is over four metres high. Hepworth made it for people to walk on and climb through.

This sculpture was created in 1966. How long ago was that?

holes

Four-Square (Walk Through), 1966

Fame and honours

From the 1950s, Barbara Hepworth became more famous. In 1965 she was given an important honour by the Queen. From then on, she was known as Dame Barbara.

Dame Barbara with her daughters outside Buckingham Palace, London.

Dame Barbara

daughters

Single Form, 1962–63

sculpture

This sculpture can be found outside the United Nations building in New York, USA.

Barbara was given many special **commissions**. Her **sculptures** were put in public places where people could see them every day.

27

A tragic end

Sadly, Hepworth died in a fire at her **studio** on 20 May 1975. She was 72 years old. She is buried in St Ives, and this **sculpture** stands nearby.

The sculpture near Hepworth's grave.

The next year, the Barbara Hepworth Museum and Sculpture Garden was opened at her old studio. Today, you can visit the place where Barbara worked. You can see many of her sculptures, just as she wished.

Hepworth often made slender upright forms rather like totem poles. Can you see shapes like that in this photograph?

upright forms

Barbara Hepworth Museum and Sculpture Garden.

Timeline

1903	Barbara Hepworth is born in Wakefield, Yorkshire on 10 January.
1914	Barbara attends Wakefield Girls' High School.
1914–18	World War I.
1920	Barbara attends Leeds School of Art.
1921	She enters the Royal College of Art, London.
1924	She visits Italy, where she learns to carve in stone.
1925	Barbara Hepworth marries John Skeaping while in Italy.
1926	Barbara and John return to London and set up **studios** there.
1928	Barbara holds her first joint **exhibition** with John.
1929	Her son, Paul, is born.
1931	Barbara meets Ben Nicholson, who later becomes her second husband.
1934	She gives birth to triplets.
1939	World War II begins. Hepworth moves to St Ives in Cornwall.
1945	World War II ends.
1949	Hepworth buys Trewyn Studio in St Ives.
1950s	She has exhibitions in New York, Venice and London.
1965	She is made 'Dame Barbara Hepworth' by the Queen.
1975	She dies in a fire in her studio on 20 May.
1976	The Barbara Hepworth Museum and Sculpture Garden is opened in her old studio.

Glossary

abstract art   art that tries to show ideas rather than the way things look

bronze   a type of metal

commission   request to make a piece of art

exhibition   public showing of art

gallery   room or building where works of art are shown

Henry Moore   famous British sculptor born in 1898

inspire   give ideas to

landscape   the countryside

marble   a type of stone which can be carved and polished

mould   hollow form for making sculptures

operating theatre   room in a hospital where operations are carried out

sculptor   artist who works in stone, wood, clay or other materials

sculpture   work of art made of stone, wood or other materials

sketch   drawing an artist does quite quickly

studio   room or building where an artist works

textures   the different ways that the surfaces of different things feel

---

More books to read

Famous Lives: Artists, Jillian Powell, Hodder Wayland

How Artists Use Pattern and Texture, Paul Flux, Heinemann Library

Website

www.tate.org.uk/stives/hepworth

More sculptures by Barbara Hepworth to see

Kneeling Figure, Wakefield City Art Gallery, Wakefield

Winged Figure, John Lewis Dept Store, Oxford St, London

a b c d e f g h i j k l m n o p q r s t u v w x y z

31

Index